SPOTLIGHT ON

# The Grand Place of Brussels

SPOTLIGHT ON

# The Grand Place of Brussels

de rouck
Publishing

## TABLE OF CONTENTS

Belgian chocolates
Belgian home

# I. INTRODUCTION



As the geographical, historical and commercial heart of Belgium, the Grand Place, is one of the most important tourist attractions in the country. But what Victor Hugo calls "the world's most beautiful market place" is not merely an impressive collection of façades. It is a living witness and custodian of history, marked with centuries of axioms and engravings, motifs and signs. It's the meeting place of patron saints, symbols and celebrities, a living theatre that has overseen the passage of governors, kings and emperors, executions and religious processions, guilds and revolutionaries, but which has also acted as a meeting point for the people of the city for nearly a millennium. Both meeting place and seat of power, the Grand Place is distinguished by its fantastic architecture and richness of history. But its importance is also revealed in the deep attachment of the people of the city to what has become an issue of identity, and their tireless determination to restore and maintain it despite bombings, fires and the grinding passage of time.

Window of *Le Cornet* framed by navigational instruments

## II. IMPORTANT DATES IN BELGIAN HISTORY

**500 BC**: Celts settle the area.

**58-50 BC**: roman invasion.

**5th century**: fall of the Western Roman Empire.

**5th-8th century**: merovingian Dynasty. Domination by the Franks (Germanic).

**8th century**: carolingian Dynasty. Charlemagne crowned Emperor by the Pope, becoming the first Germanic sovereign of the Holy Roman Empire.

**9th (843)-14th century**: the Treaty of Verdun divides the Empire among three grandsons of Charlemagne. Lothar inherits the median territory. Upon his death, his kingdom will again be divided in three: Italy, Burgundy and Lotharingia, the area of Belgium now located east of the Scheldt. Within those groups, these more or less independent political entities are rapidly established. Among them, covering what would become Belgium, the County of Flanders (Vassal of France), the Duchy of Brabant (including Brussels) and the Principality of Liège.

**From the 10th century**: the economic and population growth of these territories encouraged the development of a new class of merchants and artisans who often depended on maritime and river trade. It was at that time that cities like Bruges, Ghent, Namur, Liège and Brussels developed, becoming the first cities of the Duchy of Brabant.

**14th-15th century (1384-1482)**: burgundian period. Philippe le Hardi, Duke of Burgundy, married the heir of the County of Flanders. Brussels, the capital of Burgundy since 1430, became a first rank administrative and cultural centre. Having extended their possessions by marriage, inheritance, conquest or purchase, the Dukes of Burgundy reunited the territories of the future Belgium (excluding the Principality of Liège) under the authority of one sovereign.

**15th century**: 1482 saw the death of Mary of Burgundy, wife of the future Holy Roman Emperor Maximilian of Habsburg. The future Belgium moved to the House of Habsburg (or House of Austria).

**15th-18th century (1482-1713)**: spanish period. The grandson of Maximilian of Habsburg, Emperor Charles V (1500-1558), born in Ghent and crowned in Brussels, reunited the territories of the Holy Germanic Empire, Burgundy and Spain. The Southern Netherlands, the central government of which Brussels holds the seat, passed to the crown of Spain, until the beginning of the 18th century.

**18th century (1713-1795)**: austrian period. Following the Spanish war of succession and the hostilities between Spain and French King XIV, ending in the destruction of Brussels in 1695 and a French invasion in 1701, the Spanish Netherlands (including Belgium) passed from the Spanish Habsburgs to the Austrian Habsburgs under the Treaty of Utrecht. It was a period of overall prosperity, but it was not without its dissenters. This consolidated the central power of Brussels, which became one of the most refined cities in Europe.

**18th-19th century (1795-1814)**: in a revolutionary climate, the young French Republic invaded Brussels in 1794, and after a four-year military occupation, annexed Belgium.

**1815**: Napoléon I was defeated in Waterloo, followed by the Congress of Vienna during which the territory of Belgium was placed under the authority of King William I of Holland by Europe's great powers, in order to form a buffer state to contain French expansionist inclinations.

**1830**: an insurrection, fuelled by Catholics and liberals, who were hostile to the tutelage of Holland, resulted in the independence of Belgium.

Mary of Burgundy, *Maison du Roi*

KELDERKE
KELDERKE

The Senne, at the heart of Saint-Géry islet

# III. HISTORICAL BACKGROUND



## Brussels' origins

Brussels is often said to have had its beginnings some time in the year 979, around the time when the region was ruled by Charles, descendant of Charlemagne, Duke of Lower Lorraine and Vassal of Otto II, Emperor of the Holy Roman Empire. According to that version, Duke Charles had built a fort (or *castrum*) on a small island on the Senne (now arched) in order to keep an eye on the neighbouring Count of Flanders, Vassal of the French King. However, this date is disputed by some historians who believe that Brussels' origins can most reliably be dated back to around 1020. This version points to evidence of a small harbour on one side of the Senne, at the crossroads of a trade route that stretched from the Scheldt and the Rhine. Whether the site hosted a fort, a port or even, as some sources say, a chapel, the location of the future city —which had already hosted Neolithic settlements, Roman villas and Merovingian farms— would prove an advantage during the agricultural, urban and commercial development that would take place in Europe from the 11th century.

Starting from the 12th century, when the Counts of Louvain—and future Dukes of Brabant—moved to Brussels, the city became an important stop on the trade route between Bruges and Cologne. Protected by an enclosure four kilometres long, the city featured a princely palace on the site of today's Royal Quarter (Coudenberg), along with a chapter of secular canons devoted to St. Michael and St. Gudula. While artisans were concentrated in the district of *Notre-Dame de la Chapelle*, the area surrounding St. Nicholas's church slowly became a commercial area and a market place that was a direct extension of the Grand Place.

**Evolution from a marsh**

The site of today's Grand Place began as a marsh, surrounded by raised sand banks. The marsh bed was dried around the 11th and 12th centuries to accommodate a market. Apart from geological evidence uncovered during reconstruction and renovation of the area, the names of the adjacent streets and the houses on the square confirm this. Indeed, *Le Cornet* (*den Horn* in Flemish) was once called *La Montagne* (*den Berg*) and *L'Arbre d'Or* was known as *La Colline* (*Hille*). We also know that *Rue de Tabora* was once known as *Rue du Marais* (*Broeckenstraat*). The position of *Rue de la Colline*, which leads off the Grand Place, corresponds to the location of the raised sand bank that bordered the marsh. The market

**The Legend of the Iris**

Considering the city's beginnings as a marshland, it is no accident that the golden iris on a blue background—the Iris of the Marsh—was to become its symbol. This flower, associated with the kings of France, had already appeared on the sceptre of the descendants of Charlemagne. According to legend, it led the Dukes of Brabant to a great victory (11th-12th centuries). While battle was raging on the marshy plains surrounding the city, the Bruxellois launched their horses into the water, knowing that where the iris grew, the depth of the water would only be a few centimetres. Their enemies, ignorant of this fact, floundered miserably in deeper waters.

Cathedral of Saints Michael and Gudula

square came to be known as *Nedermerct* (market bottom), in reference to its location in the basin of the former marsh. As the soil had been soaked in water for such a long time, the first wooden structures would be raised on stilts on foundations filled with earth. Furthermore, a predominant theory for the etymology of the name "Brussels" gives further evidence of its marshy origins. The original name of the area, *Bruocsella*, *Brucsella*, or *Broekzele*, means something close to "home (*sella*) marshes (*bruoc, bruc, Broek*)" in the Germanic language.

**The place of power**

Apart from being the economic centre of the city, the market square served a number of other functions. Originally, it was lined with stalls, as well as hostels, houses and covered markets. Starting in the 12th century, the growth in the level of the artisans' activity led tradespeople to gather together in guilds, placed under the authority of a patron saint, in order to regulate work and to ensure the protection of its members. At the same time, economic growth prompted certain cities to free themselves from the tutelage of lords and to adopt autonomous municipal bodies. In the 14th century, this resulted in the construction of a number of public buildings, most notably the *Hôtel de Ville*, symbolising the power of the cities to which the headquarters of guilds were gravitating.

The *Hôtel de Ville* was soon joined by a number of guildhalls. From the 16th century onwards, the square reflected the clash between the two rival political powers in the city at the time: the *Maison du Roi*, a symbol of princely power, and the *Hôtel de Ville*, the seat of municipal power. Just like the Agora in Athens or the Forum in Rome, the square would also become the setting for elections and political assemblies, where people's claims were heard, justice administered and executions carried out. It was the setting for religious expression as well as for patriotism, for public celebrations like processions and marriages as well as tournaments, parades and theatrical performances. In its commercial function, it was to evolve with the growth of the population, leading to a growing number of diverse markets, open air or covered, often held in halls, and for the most part situated in the immediate vicinity of the Grand Place.

Remnants of Brussels's old city walls

View of the *Maison du Roi*, *Le Heaume* and *Le Paon*

**Under the cobblestones**
In order to really be able to picture the Grand Place as it was, it is important to note that its ground surface has risen with time and successive resurfacing, so that the original pavement, dating from the 11th and 12th centuries, can be found at a depth of about four feet. Since the construction of the *Hôtel de Ville*, the ground has risen by nearly two feet, slightly distorting our perception of the building. This is particularly obvious when looking at the columns and pillars of the ground floor galleries, whose foundations are to be found about forty centimetres into the ground. Therefore, the "real" Grand Place of the past is under your feet indeed...

## A thousand years of evolution

### First developments

Having developed without planning from the 11th century, the Grand Place of Brussels came to reflect the major political and economical challenges that came with the city's expansion. However, from the 11th to the 15th century, the square, with no discernible dimensions, was nothing more than a hodgepodge of houses—mostly wooden ones—separated by alleys, gardens, and empty spaces and often situated at the end of a court or surrounded by an orchard. Though the first attempts to align the buildings dates from the 13th century, it wasn't until the end of the 17th century that the square acquired its definitive, rectangular form.

The disappearance of the swamp in the beginning in the 11th century increasingly exposed the village to enemy attacks. Behind the houses of the Grand Place, between *Rue au Beurre* and *Rue de la Tête d'Or*, a rampart of earth was raised and remained until 1694. In the 12th century, the bourgeoisie, anxious to defend itself and its property, started building stone houses (*steenen*) that would be capable of withstanding sieges. Back then, the area was defended by a ring of fortified houses. In the 14th century, with the creation of an administrative body in charge of developing roads, the square was repaved and there was an attempt to expand the square and to improve its alignment through expropriation and demolitions.

Those early attempts at urban planning were followed by a period of general beautification for the city in the 15th century. The guilds, then at their peak, were given the right to participate in the administration of the city after the 1421 revolution, and settled in the vicinity of the brand new *Hôtel de Ville*. In the 16th century, many houses were still made of wood, though stone was beginning to gain ground. The former bread market gave way to the *Maison du Roi*, which was used to accommodate the courts and the offices of the rulers. The 17th century marked a fundamental shift in the appearance of the square. Following in the footsteps of tailors and painters, the guilds began to compete with one another for originality in the reconstruction of their new stone houses.

The 1695 Bombardment

But the fruit of this building frenzy was to be reduced to ashes by the greatest disaster the city had ever seen. While France battled with Spain (on whom Brussels was dependent) for possession of its northern territories, allied forces besieged the city of Namur, occupied by the French for three years. France was incensed by this affront. Louis XIV commanded Marshal Villeroy, head of the French army in Flanders, to take action. He claimed to be acting in response to the bombing of several French ports by the British army, an ally of Spain. Brussels was the target. On the night of 13th August, canons began firing, targeting the tower of the *Hôtel de Ville*. For nearly two days, the city was bombed, and the ensuing fires destroyed an area that stretches from the *Bourse* to the site of today's *Gare Centrale* (Central Station) and *Place de la Monnaie* to *Rue des Alexiens*. There were few victims

**The French King's Cannonball**

Built in the late 12th century, the Church of St. Nicholas (*Rue de Tabora*) is an interesting attraction for the visitor, thanks to an amusing detail in paticular: a cannonball embedded in one of its interior pillars is a witness to the disaster orchestrated by Louis XIV. Hint: if you don't want to spend hours looking for it, you'll find it in the fifth pillar on the left, about three metres up!

The tower of the *Hôtel de Ville*, seen from *Place d'Espagne*

as most people had been able to flee to higher grounds. However, nearly four thousand houses and fifteen churches and convents were destroyed, nearly a third of the city. On the Grand Place, however, the *Hôtel de Ville* was relatively spared along with some of the façades of the houses on the western side. The rest of the square and the city centre were almost completely devastated, along with the City's archives and numerous works of art. This act of destruction, as pointless as it was unjustified, provoked the outrage of European powers.

The reconstruction of the city, starting less than a week after the disaster, presented the opportunity to correct and extend the city streets. Plans were submitted for approval by municipal authorities and regulations were enforced to prohibit the use of thatch and wood in favour of brick and stone. Showing off the speed of their reconstruction, the façades of the Grand Place are marked with the dates of their reconstruction: 1696, 1697, 1698, 1699, 1704, 1710... And though the Golden Age was now behind them, the guilds spared no expense in replacing their burnt wooden houses with prestigious new stone ones, even embellishing them with gold. Within a few years, the Grand Place had been reborn in the guise we know today.

## Degradation and restoration

The houses built in the aftermath of the bombing deteriorated quite rapidly during the 18th century, particularly because the guilds, now in decline, no longer had the resources necessary for their maintenance. In 1793-1794, the French *sans-culottes* completed the ruin of what remained of the statues and decorations and wrecked the guild houses' meeting rooms, throwing furniture out of the windows and destroying everything considered symbolic of the inequalities of the old regime. Confiscated and nationalised, the guildhalls were sold off, and their new owners began to neglect or even get rid of their costly ornamentation.

Fortunately, in 1830, the year Belgium gained its independence, the City recognised the need to protect the square from complete ruin. The City even began to take the lead in the restoration of some of the buildings, declaring their ambition to restore the original façades as early as 1852. In 1853, the demolition of *L'Étoile* shook the collective conscience: this was to be the final significant visual

Façade of *Le Cygne*

assault committed against the square. Between 1883 and 1923, some twenty houses were restored in depth, based on plans and illustrations from the period. Under the leadership of Mayor Charles Buls, the City agreed to maintain the façades now at its own expenses, provided landlords contribute a small fee.

## An idealised past

At the close of the 19th century, there was a deliberate sense of romantic nostalgia involved in the renovations of the houses of the Grand Place. In search of its roots, and eager to encourage an emerging sense of belonging to the nation after gaining its independence, the young Belgium began to take a fresh look at its heritage. The country's identity and artistry came to be at the forefront of pressing contemporary issues.

Inspired by the work of French architect Eugène Viollet-le-Duc and the movement for the restoration of medieval heritage with its strong, Gothic revival influence, the team in charge of renovating the façades of the Grand Place interpreted the past in a very idealised way. Relying on old prints and drawings, themselves subject to a certain level of subjectivity, architect Victor Jamaer and archivist Alphonse Wauters made judgements as to the intentions of the original designers, embellishing the renovated constructions with perhaps an excessive addition of statues and ornaments. It was also during that time that most of the nameplates, cartouches and chronograms, destroyed by time and by revolutionaries, were recreated.

While some were quick to cry foul at the liberties taken in relation to history, this extensive renovation had an unexpected consequence: all projects were conducted in the same spirit by the same architects, while sculptures are the work of artists from of the Academy of Fine Arts in Brussels, giving an overall harmonising effect.

Charles Buls fountain on *Rue du Marché aux Herbes*

## The Grand Place today

Listed as a Unesco world heritage site since 1998, the Grand Place and its immediate surroundings are designated as an area of special protection. A morning market lasted until 1959 and a small flower market endures to this day. The original purpose of the square is reflected in its Dutch name, *Grote Markt*, meaning “big market”. With a size of 110 x 68 metres, it is still the heart of the city, and it hosts events and celebrations of all sorts. Each summer, the square sees the celebration of *Ommegang*, an event inspired by the folk processions of the Middle Ages, particularly the procession in honour of Charles V in 1549. For one weekend in August (in even years), a giant multi-coloured carpet made up of 750,000 flowers is laid out in the square. The *Hôtel de Ville* is also used as the setting for weddings of the royal family, along with certain locals.

Flower Market on the Grand Place

VISIT

The *Maison des Brasseurs* and its colossal columns, adorned with golden grain and hops

# IV. ARCHITECTURAL CHARACTERISTICS OF HOUSES IN THE GRAND PLACE

Though the buildings in the square may appear to constitute a harmonious whole, they are not all necessarily of the same style or time. The various styles, which can often be seen on one single façade, are the result of a syncretism of architectural styles from the Middle Ages to the 19th century. Nevertheless, the style that was applied to the houses following the bombing of 1695 is largely based on the Italian Baroque that spread throughout Europe in the 17th and 18th centuries. A descendant of the classical Renaissance, this style is characterised by its *plein cintre* arches and pilasters surmounted by capitals, but also by its decorative extravagance.

The work of Flemish architects of the period was characterised by an even freer style that experts have dubbed "Baroque Brabant".

The triangular gable of the traditional Flemish house has generally been maintained, and is often the focus of much of the ornamentation, though the sloped sawtooth and steps of the Middle Ages gave way to volutes. Also note the use of the single order or colossal order, the pillar through several floors of a house, like the Italian palaces of the Renaissance (see [10], [13]-[19] and [24]-[25]).

In the aftermath of the bombing, a French influence also started to be seen, as shown by the decoration of the gable of the *Renard* and the overall design of the *Cygne*.

The general appearance of most houses, which have the same characteristics as the traditional Brussels house, is less noticeable. Though wood completely gave way to stone after the 1695 bombardment, prominent vertical and horizontal beams are reminiscent of the timbered mansions of the 17th century.

But there is an even older discernible influence: the houses in the northeast side of the square (see [20], [21]-[22], [35]-[38]) reveal a kinship with the timber-framed houses from the medieval period.

The "skeleton" reinforcement of many façades seems to remind of the Gothic. Finally, the position of the houses on long and narrow plots is directly inherited from the Middle Ages and it is crucial to this type

**How many houses do you see?**
To the untrained eye, the square appears to encompass 25 different façades, including the *Hôtel de Ville* and the *Maison du Roi*, while excluding those houses that are clearly visible from the square but considered to belong to adjacent streets (such as the corner of *Rue de la Colline* and *Rue des Chapeliers*). But this figure does not correspond to reality. A closer look will reveal that in certain cases what appears to be a single façade actually hides between two (see [2]-[3], [21]-[22], [24]-[25], [26]-[27], [36]-[37]) and seven houses (see [13]-[19]). The reason behind this was not only cost-efficiency, but because the bigger the façade, the more beautiful it was considered to be.

Doric, Ionic and Corinthian orders on the facade of *La Rose*

of construction: buildings are developed so that the shared walls act as support, not the pine façade gables. As for the ridge of the roof, it is perpendicular to the gable, giving its triangular shape, characteristic of the northern cities of Europe.

**Guilds, yes, but not all**

It is customary to speak of the guild houses of the Grand Place as though all the buildings had served the same purpose. This impression is reinforced by the restorations of the 19th century which, considering the history of guilds to be a matter of national pride for the new Belgian State, accentuated the signs of their past prominence, including the addition of nameplates associated with the guild.

A closer look reveals that in fact only a third of the buildings were built and fully occupied by guilds. Most were simple, private houses with residents, designated for all kinds of commerce.

1697
CHOCOLAT
CHOCOLAT

*La Renommée* at the top of *Le Roi d'Espagne*

# V. HOUSES OF THE GRAND PLACE



**NB** Most houses of the Grand Place were rebuilt or restored after the bombing of 1695. In order not to overload the text with dates, they will be included only when they are of particular interest.

## Between *Rue au Beurre* and *Rue de la Tête d'Or* (west, 1-7)

### 1 Le Roi d'Espagne (The King of Spain)

¶ Reconstructed / restored: 1898-1902

In the 12th and 13th centuries, this was the site of a fortified dwelling or *steen*. Destroyed during the bombardment with the exception of its subsurface, it was rebuilt as two houses which gradually became one. Its façade suffered significant damage over time. It was entirely rebuilt in the 19th century, not without taking some liberties from its original style. The former home of the guild of bakers—one of the richest guilds in the city—it is fairly standard in its basic design, though it betrays very Italo-Flemish ornamentation: trophy, dome, corbels, the frame of the entrance door etc. Lacking the documents describing the exact appearance of the original sculptures, Mayor Charles Buls would make the decisions regarding their appearance.

In keeping with the theme of baking, the upper railing features in this order: Foresight (represented by Minerva) sowing wheat; Wind spinning mills; Water (Neptune) germinating seeds and kneading the dough; Fire cooking the bread; Strength (Hercules), without which nothing is possible, and finally

Saint-Aubert, patron saint of bakers

**The House of the Belgian Chocolate Masters**

You'll find signs for Neuhaus, Godiva and Corné all over the square, along with many other chocolate shops of varying quality. This one, however, is distinguished by its selection of chocolates made by high-level craftsmen whose goods have remained Belgian-owned, resisting interests from big international brands. *Grand Place 4, daily from 10:00 to 22:00.*

Wheat, represented by Ceres, the Goddess of agriculture who taught men how to make bread. The bronze bust above the entrance represents St. Aubert, patron saint of bakers.

Between the balusters on the first floor, there are medallions representing the emperors under whose reign their dominions flourished. They are Marcus Aurelius, Nerva, Trajan and Decius. On the second floor, the bust of King Charles II of Spain is surrounded by guns and two prisoners, a Moor and an Indian, with a particularly laudatory inscription: *Haec statuit pistor Victricia signa trophæi quo Carolus plena laude secundus ovat* ("The Baker placed the emblems of the victory trophy by which Charles II triumphed in glory"). This inscription, a chronogram, features the year 1697 in Roman numerals. In the 19th century, the golden dancing statue *Renommée* took the place of the *Victoire* at the summit.

Nowadays, the house is home to a pleasant brewery-cum-pub.

**2–3 La Brouette (The Wheelbarrow)**

¶ Restored: 1894-1913

Also known as the home of *graissiers* (grease sellers), who had been established there since 1439, this 1644 stone house was mostly spared in the bombardment. Only its ground floor and first two floors needed to be restored, though the gable and the interior were completely rebuilt. The entrance door is topped with the image

*La Brouette* and *Le Sac*

Bas-relief of *Le Sac*

*La Louve*, with its four allegories and medallions of Roman emperors

of a wheelbarrow. The façade boasts an original, antique style, the columns of the first floor feature angels and those of the second feature equally unorthodox twists. On the gable, a statue of St. Gilles, patron saint of the *graissiers*, sits. The inscriptions "*'t Vettewariershuys*" and "*den Cruywagen*" mean "House of Graissiers" and "the Wheelbarrow".

### 4 Le Sac (The Bag)

¶ Restored: 1854-1858, 1907-1913

The name of this house is indicated by a bas-relief above the entrance door. It shows a figure holding a bag into which another is dipping his hand. Partially spared in the 1695 bombardment, the building underwent a slight restoration of its lower floors while the rest was completely rebuilt. This explains why the lower parts, corresponding to the house in 1644, have a fairly sober style, while the top floor and the gable tend towards decoration that is characteristic of a later period. Originally housing a tavern, in 1644 it became the headquarters of the guild of coopers, carpenters, joiners and turners, who also rented space to other local guilds.

Like its neighbour *La Brouette*, *Le Sac* boasts a rather unrestrained Brabant-Baroque style, featuring a succession of classical influences. In addition to garlands, gastropod shells, balusters and torchères, there are also columns of accentuated relief, which become caryatids by the third floor. The balusters are decorated with reliefs depicting the tools of carpenters' and coopers' trade, such as a crankshaft, square, chisels, saw, hammer, compass etc.

### 5 La Louve (The She-Wolf)

¶ Reconstructed/restored: 1690-1691, 1696/1890-1892

Named *Le Loup* (the Wolf) in the 14th century, this house was acquired in the 17th century by the Guild of Archers of Saint Sebastian, and renamed *La Louve* (the She-Wolf), alluding to the legendary (and more prestigious) wolf of Rome. Like other houses in this block, a stone house used to stand in this location circa 1645. Following a fire in 1690, it was rebuilt and this reconstruction served as a model for its later restoration.

On the door, the hallmarks of the guild are carved into the wood: quiver, arrows, bows, swords, halberds and gloves. Motifs associated with archery and crossbow appear between the triglyphs of the first floor: helmet, arm bands, armour, target, bell and gloves. Above the door, a sculpture shows the she-wolf suckling Romulus and Remus. On the first floor, the balcony seems to equate the guild with ancient mythology, displaying the lyre and the quiver, attributes of Apollo. With its Renaissance elements (Doric pilasters, entablature and cornices), this floor somewhat contrasts with the late Baroque style of the rest of the house.

On the second floor, four sculptured allegories accompanied by Latin inscriptions seem to provide advice for the good governance of the guild with regards to political power:

- Naked truth holds an open book next to an eagle, the only bird that can look directly at the sun—*Hic Verum* means "Here the Truth";

- Falsehood has the face of a woman holding a mask, at whose feet a fox lies—*Hinc Falsum* translates to "Here the Falsehood";

- Peace is accompanied by doves and depicts a ray of unity —*Pax sit* is understood to mean "Let there be Peace";

- Discord has hair tangled with snakes and holds a torch in her hand, in front of two dogs fighting over a bone—*Discordia longe* means "Let discord be banished".

On the floor above, four medallions depict Roman emperors and are accompanied by symbolic carvings evoking the kingdoms under which these values triumphed. Truth is associated with Trajan, above a relief depicting a sun and a sunflower. Falsehood is associated with

Tiberius, above a birdcage, a net and a mask. Peace is incarnated by Augustus, above a globe surrounded by olive branches, and Discord is associated with Caesar and a relief on which two torches clash under a bleeding heart.

Other inscriptions found between floors resonate with these allegories, *firmamentum imperii* ("the support of the Empire"), *insidiae status* ("the pitfalls of the State"), *salus generis humanii* ("the salvation of mankind") and *eversio respublicae* ("the overthrow of the state").

On the last floor, the tympanum of the pediment is occupied by the figure of Apollo killing the Python with his bow. Finally, at the top, a golden phoenix rises from the flames, alluding to the fact that the house itself "rose" several times like the mythical bird, as declared by the Latin inscription on the gable: *Combusta insignior resurrexi expensis Sebastianae Guldae* ("Consumed, I will rise again more glorious under the guardianship of the Guild of Sebastian").

## 6 Le Cornet (The Cone)

¶ Restored: 1885-1902, 1987-1990

First called *den Berg* (the Mountain), this house was renamed *Le Cornet* in 1434, as indicated by the gilded sign situated above the ground floor. The first stone façade, dating from 1641-1645, was only partially destroyed in the bombardment. Rebuilt by the boatmen's guild, it is now one of the most original in the square, pushing the Italian-Flemish style to its height, keeping only traces of its tripartite division.

At each level, only the central window is flat: those on both sides have been integrated into convex or concave portions, giving a broader look to the building. Some attribute this method to the influence of the trade of its designer, cabinetmaker Antoine Pastorana. On the second floor, the pilasters were abandoned. There, the windows are framed by navigational instruments such as sailing, rigging and rudder and are dominated by the stars: the sun, the moon and two stars, one of which represents a cart, the other dogs, without doubt in reference to the constellations.

The higher levels are set on an ocean, evoked by a carved cornice of droplets that masterfully evokes the marine world. In the centre, a triton emerges riding a fish surrounded by two sea horses with webbed feet and mounted by riders, one of which used to hold a trident and the other blowing a horn, a nod to the name of the house.

More remarkable still, the cabinetmaker designed the gable like a ship's stern in the fashion of the 17th century. Its upper window arches are rippled and topped by ornamentation referencing the oceanic world. On the gable, a medal of Charles II of Spain is surrounded by four cherubs, representing the four winds, and is framed by two sailors. At the top, a shield is flanked by two lions, taking up the arms of Spain.

*Le Cornet*

*Le Renard*, *Pondere et mensura*

## 7 Le Renard (The Fox)

¶ Restored: 1770, 1879-1885

This house, whose name goes back to the 14th century, was acquired by the guild of haberdashers in the 15th century. Only the basement and ground floor, built with stone in 1641, survived the bombing.

Between the ground floor and the floor above, the bas-reliefs probably are the oldest elements of the façade. It is possible that they formed part of the house in 1641 and were then integrated into the façade of 1699, together with the year. Typical of the 17th century, it illustrates the activities of haberdashers in a simplistic way: trade of fabrics and trimmings, dyeing and manufacture of ceramics.

The first floor is festooned with allegorical sculptures. In the centre, impartial justice with eyes blindfolded, symbolises honesty, the supposed character of merchants. Around her, four statues refer to the four continents known at that time and from which the goods sold by the haberdashers came. Above, the words *Pondere et mensura* ("By weight and measure") reinforce the central allegory. At the top, a statue of St. Nicholas, patron saint of merchants, presides.

## Between *Rue de la Tête d'Or* and *Rue Charles Buls* (south-west)

## L'Hôtel de Ville (City Hall)

*The dazzling fantasy of a poet, fallen from the head of an architect.*
Victor Hugo

This building, the most imposing of the Grand Place, is also the oldest, having been built in three successive phases between 1402 and 1455. A worthy ambassador for the flamboyant Gothic style, it was supposed to embody recently acquired municipal power at a time when many public buildings were being erected. Targeted in the 1695 bombardment, the interior and the roof were destroyed by fire, though its structure was miraculously spared.

The right wing was built later than the left wing and is shorter as a result. It was constructed at a time when houses blocked the extension and made alignment with the left wing impossible. There are other features that distinguished the two wings, such as the width of the archways, the shape of windows and their ornamentation.

In the 19th century, the staircase of the Lions, which corresponded to the original entrance and once opened onto the square, was radically altered in order to be accessible through

**The Middle Ages in technicolour**

Though we might be unaware of it, our perception of some of the buildings on the square is based on the prevailing fashion of the 19th century, when triumphant neoclassicism imposed the ideal of a "bare" city of white stone. Therefore, a certain amount of imagination is required to appreciate the reality of the Middle Ages in which painting invaded architecture, colouring columns and capitals, arches and ribs vaults, enhancing the window frames and sometimes invading the walls. Lack of maintenance and changing tastes mean those murals have almost completely disappeared. However, if you look closely, traces of colour can be found in some places, like the statues of the prophets and the consoles of the big gate preserved in the Museum of the City.

the gallery. The architect Jamaer rearranged the stairs in two flights, accentuated the ornamentation and then decorated the corbels (located above the staircase) with legends from the medieval period.

The archways on the ground floor once housed merchant stalls. The Gothic-shaped arches are decorated with cabbage leaves, characteristic of Brabant Gothic motif that can also be found on the *fleurons* that cap the arches. The top of the pillars is decorated with statues of knights and squires of the seven noble houses of Brussels, the latter being privileged bourgeois who, in the old regime, had been involved in the management and protection of the city.

The gallery on the right wing reveals a particularly rich iconography through scenes illustrated on its capitals. It was realised later that those enigmatic motifs simply were a cryptic allusion, in the manner of a rebus, to the names of the three houses that were expropriated and demolished on this location: *Scupstoel* (*scup* means "shovel" and *stoel* "chair"), *Papenkeldere* ("cellar of the monks"), and *De Moer* ("The Moor"). The same themes are repeated on the keystones and sculpted corbels.

At the base of the belfry, a Gothic portal framed by eight statues of prophets is surmounted by a tympanum representing the patron saints of oaths (the protective forces

A capital alluding to the house *Scupstoel* ("shovel" and "chair")

**Why do the houses have names?**

This tradition dates back to the Middle Ages when most people were illiterate. In order to be able to identify the houses, which were not numbered, a sign was often placed above the door in the form of either a sculpture or a bas-relief. These signs often referred to the name of the first owner, to the original topography of the area or the activity that took place inside the premises.

of the city); in the centre is St. Michael, patron of swordsmen and of the city, stands; on the right, St. George, patron saint of crossbowmen and St. Gery, in whose honour the first church of the city was erected; then to the left, St. Christopher, patron of musketeers and St. Sebastian, patron saint of archers. On both sides of this portal, the allegorical statues of the four cardinal virtues stand, supported by ornaments: *Prudentia* (Prudence) and *Justitia* (Justice) on the left, *Fortitudo* (Force) and *Temperantia* (Temperance) on the right.

The sculptures of the galleries of the ground floor and the gate are 19th century copies of a set dating from the first half of the 15th century. The originals are preserved in the Museum of the City (*Maison du Roi*). Conversely, the other 294 sculptures on the façade are 19th century additions, incorporated into niches and with no other purpose than to emphasise the verticality and the relief of the building. Among the characters depicted, one finds princes (on the side of the square), mayors (*Rue Charles Buls*) and artists and scholars of Brussels (on the side of the *Rue de la Tête d'Or*).

On the first floor, a forum, common to city halls of those days, was used for official declarations. In contrast to the defensive constructions of the Middle Ages, the different levels display a spirit of openness which is particularly reflected by an abundance of windows and narrow trumeaux. At the base of the roof, however, a baluster in an aesthetic and light fashion acts as a reminder of the defensive niches of the old fortified houses of the square.

**Timeline for restorations**
In the courtyard, clear stones dating from the 19th century stone alongside a darker yellow stone, belonging to the original cladding, offer a kind of index of the restorations that were carried out here in the 19th century, as well as an indication of their magnitude.

The 97 meter high tower, assumed to be the work of Jan van Ruysbroeck, is composed of four floors adorned with turrets, piers, balconies, bay windows and corbels. It is a masterpiece of Gothic architecture, built between 1449 and 1454. Its light, openwork spire is topped by a monumental copper weathervane depicting St. Michael slaying the devil. This is a 1996 copy, and the original is kept at the *Hôtel de Ville*. Proudly towering at five meters and weighing 800 pounds, this is one of the largest weathervanes in the world. Astonishingly, the tower is not centred in the middle of the building, nor is it aligned with the entrance door on the ground floor. This asymmetry gave rise to a persistent legend according to which the architect, possibly having been deceived by the devil, hung himself, or rather, was thrown off the tower after realising his mistake.

The building at the rear, which was built later and in the style of Louis XIV, is a U-shaped extension that was added in 1706-1711 on the site of the old cloth market. In the courtyard, the two fountains are topped with allegories of the Scheldt and the Meuse rivers, dating from the 18th century, while in its centre a star marks the symbolic centre of Brussels.

**Visit the Hôtel de Ville**
A visit to the *Hôtel de Ville* offers a glimpse of the rooms, galleries, salons and hallways of the building, all decorated with pictures of old Brussels, busts and ancient tapestries that mostly date from the 18th century and whose style ranges from Gothic to Louis XIV. For more information, visit the Information Desk of VisitBrussels located on the ground floor of the right wing (see p. 92).

## Between *Rue Charles Buls* and *Rue des Chapeliers* (south-east, 8-12)

### 8 L'Étoile (The Star)

¶ Reconstructed / restored: 1897, 2008

This modest house, destroyed in 1853 in order to expand access to the square, was eventually rebuilt, almost in its original form, in 1897, with the exception of the ground floor, which was replaced by an archway. The name has been known since 1299. In the Middle Ages, it was occupied by the amman, the magistrate who represented the Duke. It was then private property, annexed by *Le Cygne* as a restaurant and finally bought by the City in the 19th century.

Under the archway, a memorial monument in the Art nouveau style dating from 1899 is the work of Victor Horta and Victor Rousseau. It is dedicated to Charles Buls, the mayor who devoted himself in earnest to the renovation projects of the square, as well as to the architects who participated in its construction.

### 9 Le Cygne (The Swan)

¶ Restored: 1895-1904, 2008

This Louis XIV-style façade of this house, whose name dates back to the 14th century, was originally built for banker Pierre Fariseau, whose monogram appears in its centre. In 1720, the

*L'Étoile* and *Le Cygne*

**A recumbent figure brings good luck**
Under the arcade of *L'Étoile*, you'll find a 1902 work by Julien Dillens, a copper statue dedicated to Evrard t'Serclaes, a 14th century Brussels hero who defended the rights of the people of the city against the Lord of Gaasbeek. Assaulted by the latter's men, he was moved into this house where he died in 1388. The three bas-reliefs located above the recumbent figure illustrate the retaking of the city by the people of Brabant, the arrival of the Dukes of Louvain Jeanne and Wenceslas, and the assassination of t'Serclaes. According to tradition, rubbing different parts of the sculpture in a set order makes one's wish come true.

building became the property of the butchers' guild until its being nationalised in 1798. Karl Marx and Friedrich Engels took part in meetings of the German Workers' Party there, along with Jules Vallès and members of the Belgian Labour Party, which was in all likelihood founded there in 1885.

With a classic Louis XIV-style, typical of the medieval period, the façade, virtually devoid of pilasters, is distinguished by a large pediment and a greater balance between full and empty spaces (where most houses seem to be made up of the maximum possible number of windows). Abandoning the traditional gable, the imperial roof is topped by a decorative lookout while displaying a baroque inspiration in its decor, which features symbols of Abundance, Agriculture and Butchery.

### 10 L'Arbre d'Or (The Golden Tree) / La Maison des Brasseurs

¶ Restored: 1893-1900, 2008

Called *La Colline* from 1299 onwards, probably in reference to its topographical location on the sandbank, which bordered the old raised marsh, this house became known as the *Arbre d'Or* in 1523 and the *Maison des Brasseurs* in 1638. It was the headquarters of the tanners guild in the 15th century, followed by the upholsterers', until it passed into the hands of the brewers early in the 17th century and remained there until it was nationalised in 1798.

Today, the house has somewhat returned to its roots; it became the headquarters of the Professional Association of Belgian Brewers in 1954.

*La Maison des Brasseurs* and *La Rose*

**Museum of Belgian Brewers**

Today, the cellar of this house hosts a small Belgian Brewers Museum, presenting ancient artefacts and a short film on the craft of brewing. You can enjoy a beer in the small adjoining tavern.
*Grand Place 10, Monday to Sunday from 10:00 to 17:00.*

The façade of this house features something very odd. The ground floor columns feature carvings with strange motifs, which are usually interpreted as drops of water, a reference to one of the ingredients for beer. This interpretation is confirmed on subsequent floors by the colossal columns adorned with hops and ears of golden wheat. On the second floor, animated reliefs of children—an unusual pairing—describe activities related to brewing: harvesting, transporting beer and hop-picking. These reliefs probably date back to the 17th century, though they were restored several times.

On the pediment, a panegyric praising Charles of Lorraine is flanked by two lions, with two dolphins at the base of the gable seem to respond to the motions on the pedestal volutes.

### 11 La Rose (The Rose)

¶ Restored: 1884-1888, 2008

This former private residence has been known as the Rose since the 15th century. However, it is unclear whether the house was named for the family or conversely. Its typical Italian-Flemish façade superimposes the Doric, Ionic and Corinthian/Composite orders in a very simple manner, under a decorated gable.

### 12 Le Mont Thabor (Mount Thabor)

¶ Restored: 1885-1889, 2008

Known by this name since the 16th century (though also known as *Aux Trois Couleurs*), this house seems to have originally been intended for housing and commerce, which is why it has the appearance of a bourgeois abode. Despite its volutes, the jagged gable structure betrays the graded (or tiered) style of traditional Flemish architecture.

## Between *Rue des Chapeliers* and *Rue de la Colline* (east, 12a-19)

### 12a L'Alsemberg

¶ Reconstructed/restored: 1895-1908

Located on 12a of the *Rue des Chapeliers*, this house is not technically located on the square though it forms part of its visible landscape. The name of its architect, Adrien de Vleeschouwer, appears on the façade. Though it seems to have always been the property of individuals, it is known that one of its rooms was rented to a guild in the 18th century. During its renovation, Mayor Charles Buls chose the busts appearing on the façade, and it was he who decided that they should represent the constituent ingredients of beer: in the centre, Gambrinus, a legendary Flemish hero who invented beer; to the right, Ceres and Water (old bearded man) and to the left, fire (Vulcan) and hops.

Symbol of la Renommée

### 13-19 L'ensemble des Ducs de Brabant (Houses of the Dukes of Brabant)

¶ Restored: 1824-1851, 1881-1892, 1986-1990

This imposing façade actually is an ensemble of six houses and a passage that leads to a house hidden in the interior of the block. The only distinguishing feature for each of the houses is the entry door, which is surmounted by signs that identify each one (tools for sculptors and masons, a tin pot for carpenters, a mill for millers, a woman sitting on a golden wheel bearing the horn of plenty for tanners and finally a simple purse and a hermit in reference to the names of two other houses).
The day after the 1695 bombardment, Maximilian Emmanuel of Bavaria, then governor of the region, commissioned city architect Guillaume de Bruyn to build it and to impose the shared façade. In the 12th century, numbers 18 and 19 corresponded to the location of Meynaert *steen*, one of the fortified town houses which were the first stone buildings in the square. In 1441, an ensemble of six identical stone houses was built in the place of the *steen*. However, in the aftermath of the bombing, nothing remained except underpasses. This façade, which stands out for being horizontal, is made up of nineteen bays punctuated by "colossal" pilasters passing through several floors in the style of Italian Renaissance palaces, and topped with Corinthian capitals or composite capitals. In contrast, the various nameplates, busts, balusters, torchères and dormer windows remain faithful to the Italian-Flemish tradition. At the base of each pilaster, the nineteen busts represent dukes and duchesses of Brabant. An allegorical pediment added in 1770 sits at the top, symbolising abundance.

#### 13. La Renommée

Called *Den Halsberch* from 1440 until 1695, this mansion is located within the interior of the block and today, it is connected to the square by a courtyard and a passageway which has been covered since the 19th century.

#### 14. L'Ermitage (The Hermitage)

In the 17th century, this house, which had also been known as *Le Trépied* (the Tripod) and *L'Écrevisse* (the Crayfish) before the 19th century, served as headquarters to several guilds, which used to rent a meeting room there.

ANNO
1697

15. La Fortune

Called Meynaert until 1695 in reference to a *steen* of that name that once stood in this location, this house was acquired by the guild of tanners in 1759 for twenty years only. In the basement, the restaurant 't Kelderke serves typical Belgian cuisine to hungry tourists in a vaulted cellar.

16. Le Moulin à Vent (The Windmill)

Property of the City of Brussels since 1441, then privately owned until 1695, this plot was then bought by the guild of millers.

17. Le Pot d'Étain (The Tin Pot)

Since the 15th century, this house has been home to the guild of carpenters and joiners, an occupancy that lasted until it was nationalised.

## 18. La Colline (The Hill)

Known by that name since 1395, this house belonged to the guild of the Four Crowned Martyrs before 1695. That name refers to the martyrdom of Christian craftsmen who refused to make a pagan idol, as commanded by a Roman emperor. It brings four trades together: sculptors, stonemasons, bricklayers and masons. This remained their headquarters until the late 18th century, while renting rooms to other guilds.

## 19. La Bourse (The Purse)

Sold as national property in the 18th century, this house seems to have been a private property at least since 1695, and to have partly dedicated to commerce.

**Between *Rue de la Colline* and *Rue des Harengs* (north-east, 20-28)**



### 20 Le Cerf (The Stag)

¶ Reconstructed/restored: 1710, 1896-1899, 2011-2012

Alternately called *La Bourse*, *La Bourse d'Or*, *L'Arbre* and *Le Cerf Volant* before 1695, this private house was later renamed *Le Cerf*. Reminiscent of the style of 17th century bourgeois dwellings, like its neighbour *Joseph et Anne*, it is little influenced by Italian works and the arrangement of its narrow piers and its protruding bands sectioning the façade, recalls the lines of old wooden and mud houses and of mud from the distant past. The initial crow-stepped gable has evolved over time.

### 21-22 Joseph et Anne

¶ Reconstructed/restored:
1896-1899, 2011-2012

Like many others, this double house, which had already been rebuilt in stone before 1695, was probably rebuilt above its old cellars, which were partly spared by the bombing. Cartouches bear the inscriptions "Anna" and "Joseph". Heavily modified in the 19th century, the façade was eventually totally rebuilt to restore its original appearance, making it almost totally devoid of Italian influence. The two private houses were combined during the 20th century, both serving for mixed use.

### 23 L'Ange (The Angel)

¶ Reconstructed/restored:
1895-1899, 2011-2012

Though the former name of this house is *L'Olivier*, is was renamed after 1695 due to the presence of two angel-headed medallions. Having already been rebuilt in stone in 1527, it was a property of the Abbey of Forest initially, before becoming the property of private individuals. Unlike other houses previously mentioned, it is set into the Italian-Flemish tradition, as evidenced by the Ionic and Corinthian pilasters.

## 24-25 La Chaloupe d'Or (The Golden Wheelbarrow)

¶ Restored: 1879-1880, 1898-1899, 2011-2012

Like its neighbour, this house was originally conceived as two separate houses that shared the same façade. In evidence since the 14th century, its name corresponds to that of one of the two parts, the second having been named *La Taupe* (the Mole) until 1695. Though it has been headquarters to the guild of tailors since 1500, it was also rented to other guilds.

Like many others, this house blends an Italian baroque structure with Flemish ornamentation. At the top, the statue of St. Boniface stands, whereas a medallion of Saint Barbara, patron saint of tailors, is set above the door. The Latin inscription, which appears next to the date of reconstruction, declares "The house that the fury of the enemy destroyed by fire, the tailor made to rise again is and dedicated to the magistrates". This house is now home to one of the finest cafés in the square.

## 26-27 Le Pigeon

¶ Restored: 1901-1908, 2011-2012

This double house, whose name has existed since 1510, was rebuilt in stone in 1553. It began as the home of the guild of painters who, lacking resources, were forced to sell it back to the architect during reconstruction. Like most "grouped façades" on the square, it was conceived as two distinct houses. During his exile in Brussels, Victor Hugo stayed there in 1852 and it was there that he wrote the pamphlet *Napoléon the Little* addressed to Napoléon III.

Its simple and sober façade is distinguished by its windows, which abandon the rectangular, muntin design in favour of arches in *plein cintre* and a Palladian window on the first floor. Italian-inspired, it is characterised by three grouped bays made up of a central bay surmounted by a semi-circular arch and framed by two narrower lateral bays supported by a lintel.

*L'Ange*, *La Chaloupe d'Or* and *Le Pigeon*

## 28 Aux Armes de Brabant (The Brabant Arms) or La Chambrette de l'Amman

¶| Reconstructed / restored: after 1709, 1896-1899, 2011-2012

This house was formerly known as the *Le Marchand d'Or* and the *Chambrette de l'Amman*, the latter being the officer who represented the Duke of Brabant in Brussels in the 14th century. The new name dates from the 19th century and alludes to its nameplate, which is the coat of arms of Brabant. According to the archives, despite what the name "Amman Chamber" might suggest, the house never filled any administrative purpose, having always been used for housing and commerce. With a simple Baroque style, it does not comply with the classic succession of the orders, displaying a first floor with Tuscan capitals, followed by two floors in the Ionic order.

## Between *Rue des Harengs* and *Rue Chair et Pain* (north-east)

## La Maison du Roi (The King's House)

Initially built in the 16th century in the late Gothic style on the site of the old medieval bread market (*broodhuis*), this building housed the administrative offices of Charles V, from which the name originates. Though no king ever lived there, the buildings alternately served as Duke of Brabant's property, Receiver General's office, as a court and even as a jail. It was here too that the Counts of Egmont and Hornes, two local heroes who became legends in the 19th century, spent their last night before being executed in 1568 by the Spanish Inquisition. Renamed *Maison du Peuple* (House of the People) by French revolutionaries, the building was bought by a wealthy aristocrat before being sold to private individuals and, finally, to the City.

Largely destroyed during the 1695 bombardment—with the exception of the main façade and a section of a side wall—the building was not restored until 1763. Contrarily to what its style might suggest, its current appearance is the result of a total reconstruction that was carried out in the 19th century. This idealised restoration incorporated a flamboyant Gothic

**Museum of the City**
Since 1887, the *Maison du Roi* has housed the excellent Museum of the City, which brings both the historical records and works of art that have secured Brussels' reputation together. While visiting, don't miss the tiles bearing the coat of arms in the entrance hall or the staircase windows representing the symbols of Charles V's empire. The ground floor is dedicated to fine arts and decoration. Thematic exhibitions on the evolution of the city are housed on the first floor. Finally, the wardrobe of the Manneken-Pis is kept on the second floor, a collection of over eight hundred costumes of which only a hundred are on display.
*Tuesday to Sunday from 10:00 to 17:00, Thursday until 20:00*
*Tel: + 32 (0)2 279 43 50.*

revival style that was very fashionable at the time. The project, which lasted twenty-two years and cost the City a fortune, illustrates the particularly interventionist policy employed by Mayor Charles Buls. With its genuine lace stonework, the building is now considered a masterpiece of Gothic revival architecture.

The galleries on the ground floor feature a throwback to medieval polychromy, as evidenced by white stone arches joined under vaults of red brick contrasting with blue stone.

The sculptures were chosen to illustrate the history of the building through the principal sovereigns who inhabited it: Henry I, Count of Leuven and first Duke of Brabant, who granted Brussels its first charter in the 13th century; St. Jean de Brabant, called "the Victorious"; Duchess Mary of Burgundy, who gave the King's House to the City in the 15th century; and finally Charles V, who initiated the building's reconstruction in the 16th century. These last two sculptures flank the entrance.

The façade also features sculptures of a judge, a merchant, a rafter and an archer. As for the individual holding a pin topped with a chicken, it might be an allusion to the humorous nickname of Brussels, *kiekenfretters* ("chicken eaters").

At the top of the tower, crowned bread recalls the old bread market. Towards *Rue des Harengs,* diocese meetings are evoked by the figure of a monk while gentlemen symbolise the forestry tribunal, along with those of hunting and fishing. The side of the *Rue Chair et Pain*, men in arms evoke the meetings of guilds of military musketeers, crossbowmen and swordsmen.

Finally, a steep roof of Ardennes slate is topped by a ridge of iron and lead, flanked by octagonal turrets whose aerial arrows correspond to those of the *Hôtel de Ville*.

## Between *Rue Chair et Pain* and *Rue au Beurre* (north-west, 34-39)

### 34 Le Heaume (The Helmet)

¶ Restored: 1879, 1916-1923

This house, whose name can be traced back to the 15th century, has always been a private property. It served a number of different uses, though a meeting room was rented to a guild from 1695. With its tripartite division and its gable trimmed with garlands of flowers and fruit, this house fully subscribes to the Italian-Flemish Baroque style.

*Sainte-Barbe* and *L'Âne*

### 35 Le Paon (The Peacock)

¶ Restored: 1876-1895

During restoration, this fairly simple house enjoyed the reappearance of its ornamentation, frames, nameplate and date of reconstruction, as well as the original arrangement of its ground floor. Serving the same purpose as its neighbours (private lodging and commerce), its architecture too is similar. The façade features a bas-relief depicting a peacock.

### 36-37 Le Petit Renard and Le Chêne (The Little Fox and The Oak)

¶ Converted/restored: after 1749, 1883-1886

Formerly known as *L'Arbre vert* (the Green Tree) and *Le Samaritain*, these two houses were privately owned and used for housing and commerce. Little influenced by classical architecture, the façade has its origins in Brussels' houses of yesteryear, as evidenced by the prominent vertical and horizontal beams as well as its dormer windows.

## 38 Sainte-Barbe (Saint Barbara)

¶ Transformed/reconstructed: after 1749, 1913-1920

Renamed *La Ronce Couronnée* (the Crowned Bramble) in the 19th century, this house was first rebuilt in bricks, then in stone in the 20th century. As a private property, it was intended for both trade and housing. Despite its apparent simplicity, its structure and ornamentation reveal a certain amount of influence of medieval pine houses. This is particularly true for the narrow piers, which support its very characteristic "skeletal" appearance, but also its decor simply conceived as either hollowed or raised panels. The bas-relief represents St. Barbara.

## 39 L'Âne (The Donkey)

¶ Reconstructed/restored: 1913-1920, 2002-2004

This house was probably reconstructed on top of its original foundations, probably in plastered bricks to start with, then in stone in the 20th century. Private property since at least 1695, little is known about it except that it was used for both trade and housing.

# VI. USEFUL ADDRESSES

Don't hesitate to pay a visit to the **VisitBrussels Information Office** ①, located on the ground floor of the right wing of the *Hôtel de Ville*.
*Open daily from 9:00 to 18:00, Tel.: +32 (0)2 513 89 40, www.visitbrussels.be.*

## Museums and monuments

### Manneken-Pis ②

On the corner of *Rue de l'Étuve* and *Rue du Chêne*, this celebrated little personality (*manneken* meaning "little guy") is located just steps from the Grand Place. The cheerful bronze statuette was created in 1619 by Jérôme Duquesnoy. Gender equality dictates that he is joined by a companion, Jeanneke-Pis, situated near *Rue des Bouchers* (*Impasse de la Fidélité*).

### Bruxella 1238 ③

(Bourse, *Boulevard Anspach*)
For history buffs, this site exposes the buried remains of the old Franciscan convent of the Récollets, founded in 1238. You can take a look through the windows or visit the site.
*Tel.: +32 (0)2 279 43 50, bookings: + 32 (0)2 279 43 55.*

## Galeries Saint-Hubert

These magnificent neoclassical arcades, composed of the *galerie de la Reine* (Queen's), the *galerie du Roi* (King's) and the *galerie des Princes* (Princes') are considered to be the first covered galleries in Europe. Inaugurated by Leopold I in 1847, these galleries are the works of architect Jean-Pierre Cluysenaar and once were very fashionable, attracting artistic and literary circles (now *Taverne du Passage*), with lots of famous writers, among whom Victor Hugo, Charles Baudelaire, Guillaume Apollinaire and Alexandre Dumas. This is also where the Lumière brothers projected their first film. This prestigious jewel is an unmissable upscale shopping trip with shops, cafés, restaurants and even a theatre. Among them:

**- L'Ogenblik** ④: Belgian and French cuisine in a beautiful classic brasserie *à l'ancienne*.
*Galerie des Princes 1, Monday to Saturday, from 12:00 to 14:30 and from 19:00 to 0:00 (closed on Sundays), Tel.: + 32 (0)2 511 61 51.*

**- Tropismes** ⑤: excellent general French bookshop in a dream setting of mirrors, stucco and wrapped columns.
*Galerie des Princes 11 (Tel.: + 32 (0)2 512 88 52) and Galerie du Roi 4 (Tel.: + 32 (0)2 511 56 51), all week long, hours vary daily, 10:00/13:30 to 18:30/19:30.*

**- Musée des Lettres et Manuscrits** ⑥: the museum aims at enhancing the value of Belgian and international written heritage through 80,000 manuscripts, letters and other testimonies of world renowned artists and writers.
*Galerie du Roi 3, Tuesday to Sunday from 10:00 to 19:00, 20:00 on Saturday and until 21:30 on Thursday, Tel.: + 32 (0)2 514 71 87, www.mlmb.be.*

**- Arcadi Café** ⑦ : at the very end of the gallery, this warm and slightly retro café offers simple and good food, with specialities of sweet or vegetable tarts.
*Rue d'Arenberg 1b, daily non-stop serving from 7:00 to 23:30, Tel.: + 32 (0)2 511 33 43.*

L'Ogenblik

Musée des Lettres et Manuscrits

**Dandoy** ⑧⑨
Since 1829, Brussels' celebrated signature biscuits have included *speculoos*, gingerbread, *cramiques* and *pain à la grecque*, which is typically Belgian despite its name. There are two places in the neighbourhood where you can get your hands on them: *Rue Charles Buls 14*, which is also a tearoom, and the main shop on *Rue au Beurre 31. Every day from 9:30 to 18:30.*

**Boutique Tintin** ⑩
If you are passionate about the adventures of the young reporter, pay a visit to this shop for comics, clothes, gadgets and a whole range of other products. *Rue de la Colline 13, Monday to Saturday from 10:00 to 18:00 and Sundays from 11:00 to 17:00, Tel.: + 32 (0) 2 514 51 52.*

**De Biertempel** ⑪
For fans of hoppy brew, this shop offers a selection of over six hundred different beers in vessels of all shapes and sizes in a wide variety of related products.
*Rue du Marché aux Herbes 56b, daily from 10:00 to 19:00, Tel.: + 32 (0)2 502 19 06.*

**Galerie Bortier** ⑫
The atmosphere in this covered passageway is intimate and quaint. Created in 1848 by Jean-Pierre Cluysenaar, the architect of *Galeries Saint-Hubert,* it is a haven for book-lovers and old postcards and prints enthusiasts. *Rue de la Madeleine 55, access by the Rue de la Madeleine, Monday to Saturday from 10:00 to 18:30.*

Galerie Bortier

## Restaurants, cafés, bars and pubs

**Aux Armes de Bruxelles** ⑬
Excellent Belgian cuisine in a renowned brewery with old-fashioned charm. Mussels are a speciality.
*Rue des Bouchers 13, daily from 12:00 to 23:15, Tel.: + 32 (0)2 511 55 98.*

**Le Delirium Tremens** ⑭
Located in an 18th century cellar, this bar features almost 2,600 beers from around the world. Fourteen out of them are served from the tap and 1,800 Belgian ones, including some rare ones and collectible copies.
*Impasse of Fidelity 4a, Tel.: + 32 (0)2 514 44 34.*

**L'Imaige Nostre Dame** ⑮
A landmark old Brussels tavern at the bottom of a timeless lane. The house itself is one of the few that escaped the bombing of 1695 and features some lesser-known beers like St. Feuillien and the Bourgogne des Flandres on its menu. Another similar establishment, **Au Bon Vieux Temps** ⑯, is not far away (*Impasse Saint-Nicolas 15*). *Impasse des Cadeaux 3, up to the n. 8 Rue du Marché aux Herbes. Every day, flexible hours from 12:00 to 15:00, from 15:00 on Saturday and 16:00 on Sunday to 20:00 or 1:00, or depending on the day, Tel.: + 32 (0)2 219 42 49.*

**À la Bécasse** ⑰
Situated at the bottom of a dead end, this rustic tavern allegedly once frequented by Maupassant is also one of the few to serve Gueuze and Lambic beers, brews that are typical of Brussels and its surroundings.
*Rue de Tabora 11, Monday to Saturday from 11:00 to 0:00, Tel.: + 32 (0)2 511 00 06.*

**Le Cercle des Voyageurs** ⑱
A stone's throw from Manneken-Pis, this coffee shop is a beautiful enticement to travel to, with exhibitions, conferences, concerts, creative cuisine and a selection of teas.
*Rue des Grands Carmes 16-18, daily from 9:30 to 0:00 or so, Tel.: + 32 (0)2 514 39 49.*

**Brasserie de la Roue d'Or** ⑲
This is another good traditional pub, a little bit out off the beaten tracks. Set in a pleasant backdrop of dark wood under a heaven-like coloured glass skylight.
*Rue des Chapeliers 26, open daily from 12:00 to 0:00, Tel.: + 32 (0)2 514 25 54.*

Aux Armes de Bruxelles

### Le Soleil ⑳

A nice café with a pleasant terrace for a drink, a sandwich or a fresh soup, day or night near the Manneken-Pis.
*Rue du Marché au Charbon 86, open daily from 10:00 to 0:00 (2:00 on weekends), Tel.: + 32 (0)2 511 76 00.*

### L'Arrière Cuisine ㉑

A place for a good breakfast, brunch or a sweet and sour snack with a large selection of teas.
*Rue des Grands Carmes 11, Wednesday to Saturday from 10:00 to 18:30 and Sunday from 11:30 to 18:30, Tel.: + 32 (0)2 513 16 18.*

### Goupil le Fol ㉒

A slightly bohemian café decorated like an old attic where classic old French music has gone down well with fruit wines and cocktails for decades.
*Rue de la Violette 22, daily from 16:00 to 5:00, Tel.: + 32 (0)2 511 13 96.*

## Spectacles

### Théâtre Toone ㉓

Since 1830, this wonderful little puppet theatre has put on such classics as *Romeo and Juliet* and *The Three Musketeers*, mixing local dialect and French in authentic Brussels fashion. A small tavern adds to the delightful atmosphere.
*Impasse Schuddeveld 6, leading to the Petite Rue des Bouchers. Show some days at 20:30, at 16:00 on Saturday, Tel.: + 32 (0)2 513 54 86, www.toone.be*

A musketeer at the Toone Theatre

## VII. GLOSSARY

**Bay**: a general term for an opening framed by two vertical elements.

**Capital**: forms the topmost element of a column.

**Cartouche**: an ornamental stone carved with an inscription, decorating the façade of a building. It may contain a date, a name, a motto, a coat of arms or an ornamental pattern.

**Corbel**: a piece of masonry jutting out of a wall to support any super-incumbent weight, such as the base of a column, a statue or a fallen arch.

**Doric, Ionic and Corinthian classical orders**: classical orders used for the tripartite division of classical façades and identifiable mainly in ornamentation of the capitals (very simple moldings to the Doric, Ionic volutes for or acanthus leaves on Corinthian). The composite order, inspired by Roman and even heavier, combines scrolls and acanthus leaves.

**Fleuron**: ornamental plant lines ending some building parts, particularly Gothic.

Example of a cartouche

Base with Doric capital

**Lintel**: straight element, sometimes decorated, to support the masonry above a door, a window or a bay.

**Muntin**: also called mullioned window, this window type emerged in the 14th century and it is typical of the Renaissance. It is made up of a vertical band called a mullion and a cross-section dividing it perpendicularly, from mid-height to two-thirds of its height.

**Pier**: part of a wall or the area between two windows.

**Pilaster**: a square column initiated by a base and ending in a tent, projecting from a wall in which it is embedded.

**Pinnacle**: the highest part of a building, synonym of ridge.

***Plein cintre***: generally refers to a vault or an arch forming a semicircle.

Semicircular arc, amongst others

## VIII. REFERENCES

De Pange, Isabelle, *La Grand-Place de Bruxelles*, Bruxelles, Aparté, 2011.

Dessouroux, Christian, *Espaces partagés, espaces disputés. Bruxelles, une capitale et ses habitants*, Bruxelles, Université Libre de Bruxelles (CIRHIBRU) & Ministère de la Région de Bruxelles-Capitale, 2008.

Heymans, Vincent (dir.), *Les Maisons de la Grand-Place de Bruxelles*, Bruxelles, CFC Éditions, 2011.

Pujo, Nathalie (dir.), *Villes d'art de Belgique*, Paris, Hachette, 2011.

Smolar-Meynart, Ariette et Stengers, Jean (dir.), *La Région de Bruxelles. Des villages d'autrefois à la ville d'aujourd'hui*, Bruxelles, Crédit communal de Belgique, 1989.

Van Beek, Nicolas et Capart, Nathalie, *Bruxelles insolite et secret,* Versailles, Jonglez, 2008.

# COLOPHON



*Spotlight on the Grand Place of Brussels*

**De Rouck Publishing is a brand of Renaissance du Livre**

Renaissance du Livre
Avenue du Château Jaco, 1 –
1410 Waterloo
www.renaissancedulivre.be,
www.derouck.com

**Editing**: Julie Galand.
**Translation**: Rose Kelleher.
**Layout**: theatre-operations.com
**Photographs cover**:
© Croquet Anne & Philippe.
**Map**: © De Rouck Geocart.

**Photos Credits**:
© Croquet Anne & Philippe : p. 4, 9, 10-12, 15-19, 21, 23-24, 27, 29, 31, 33-37, 39-45, 47-50, 52-53, 55-57, 59, 61-63, 65, 67, 69-72, 74-76, 83, 85-93, 97, 103-105.
© Isabelle de Pange : p. 77-78, 80-81.
© L'Ogenblik : p. 95.
© Musée des Lettres et Manuscrits : p. 95.
© Aux Armes de Bruxelles : p. 99.
© Théâtre Toone : p. 101.

**Printing**: Drukkerij Smits (Belgium).

ISBN : 978-2-507-05039-9
Legal Deposit : D/2012/12.763/22

# NOTES

# NOTES

GUIDE AND MAP

# BRUSSELS

TOURIST PUBLICATION

Ref 631

de rouck geocart